They're cute! They're quick! They're so much fun, you'll want to stitch them all — then

Gail Bussi's six holiday samplers will brighten your home year-round with their friendly characters and appealing images. And you don't have to stitch an entire sampler to enjoy these seasonal designs. The individual "segments" of each one can be stitched separately for an endless number of little gifts or items for home décor. For example, you can create a bewitching bookmark with a witch or ghost for Halloween. Or fashion a candle band with a row of leaves for Thanksgiving. Show your patriotism by wearing a heart-shaped flag pin. Make an angel ornament or a Santa gift tag for Christmas. As you can see, there's no limit to all the fun you'll have while "sampling the seasons!"

Leisure Arts, Inc • Little Rock, Arkansas

Sing a Song of Liberty!
No. 152
The Star-Spangled Banner

NOEL
PEACE

Easter Blessings

X	DMC	1/4X	B'ST	ANC.	COLOR
☆	blanc	☆		2	white
2	209			109	dk lavender
#	210			108	lavender
<	211			342	lt lavender
T	320		/	215	green
◆◆	368			214	lt green
	420		/	374	brown
4	436			1045	golden brown
O	437			362	lt golden brown
	645		/	273	dk grey
e	647	e		1040	grey
△	648			900	lt grey
⧗	738	⧗		361	tan
9	743			302	dk yellow
7	744			301	yellow
8	745			300	lt yellow
H	818			23	lt pink
X	899			52	dk pink

X	DMC	ANC.	COLOR
↑	922	1003	orange
▲	3326	36	pink
L	3816	876	sea green
6	3817	875	lt sea green
m	3823	386	vy lt yellow
●	645	273	dk grey Fr. Knot

Grey area indicates last row of previous section of design.

The design was stitched on a $13^1/2$" x $10^1/4$" piece of 32 count White Linen over two fabric threads (design size $7^1/2$" x $4^1/4$"). Two strands of floss were used for Cross Stitch and one strand for Backstitch and French Knots. The design was custom framed.

Stitch Count (117w x 67h)

14 count	$8^1/2$"	x	5"
16 count	$7^1/2$"	x	$4^1/4$"
18 count	$6^1/2$"	x	$3^3/4$"

Americana Summer

X	DMC	1/4X	B ST	ANC.	COLOR
☆	blanc			2	white
S	320			215	green
T	368			214	lt green
C	369			1043	vy lt green
	420		/	374	golden brown
	535		/	401	grey
3	611			898	brown
Y	676	Y		891	gold
/	677			886	lt gold
Λ	680			901	dk gold
2	760	2		1022	pink
−	818			23	lt pink
)	930		/	1035	dk blue
▲	931	▲		1034	blue

X	DMC	1/4X	B ST	ANC.	COLOR
×	932	×		1033	lt blue
7	3328		/	1024	dk salmon
	3363		/	262	olive
O	3712			1023	salmon
L	3752			1032	baby blue
I	3753			1031	lt baby blue
a	3816			876	sea green
⌐	3817			875	lt sea green
n	3828	n		373	lt golden brown
●	535			401	grey Fr. Knot
●	3328			1024	dk salmon Fr. Knot
✳	729			890	yellow eyelets

Grey area indicates last row of previous section of design.

The design was stitched on a 14$^1/_4$" x 9$^1/_2$" piece of 32 count Natural Linen over two fabric threads (design size 8$^1/_4$" x 3$^1/_2$"). Two strands of floss were used for Cross Stitch and Algerian Eye Stitch and one strand for Backstitch and French Knots. The design was custom framed.

Stitch Count (130w x 55h)

14 count	9$^1/_2$"	x	4"
16 count	8$^1/_4$"	x	3$^1/_2$"
18 count	7$^1/_4$"	x	3$^1/_4$"

Algerian Eye Stitch: An "eye" is formed in the center of this stitch. Come up at 1, go down in center, and pull tightly toward 3. Come up at 3, go down in center, and pull tightly toward 5; continue working in this manner until stitch is complete (stitches 5-15) ***(Fig. 1)***.

Fig. 1

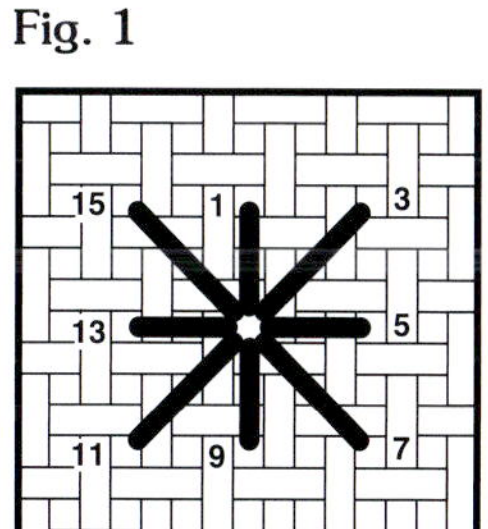

I Love Halloween

X	DMC	B'ST	ANC.	COLOR
☆	blanc		2	white
>	317		400	grey
C	413		236	dk grey
3	414		235	lt grey
#	422		943	lt tan
2	434		310	dk golden brown
<	611	/	898	tan
+	762		234	vy lt grey
◇	772		259	vy lt green
	801	/	359	brown
∞	921		1003	dk orange
9	922		1003	orange
✳	988	/	243	green
↑	3364		260	olive green
)	3799	/	236	vy dk grey
√	3821	/	305	gold
5	3822		295	lt gold
8	3825		323	lt orange
●	801		359	brown Fr. Knot
●	988		243	green Fr. Knot
●	3799		236	vy dk grey Fr. Knot

Grey area indicates last row of previous section of design.

The design was stitched on a 13 1/2" x 11 1/4" piece of 32 count Cream Linen over two fabric threads (design size 7 1/4" x 5 1/4"). Two strands of floss were used for Cross Stitch and one strand for Backstitch and French Knots. The design was custom framed.

Stitch Count (113w x 83h)

14 count	8 1/4"	x 6"
16 count	7 1/4"	x 5 1/4"
18 count	6 1/2"	x 4 3/4"

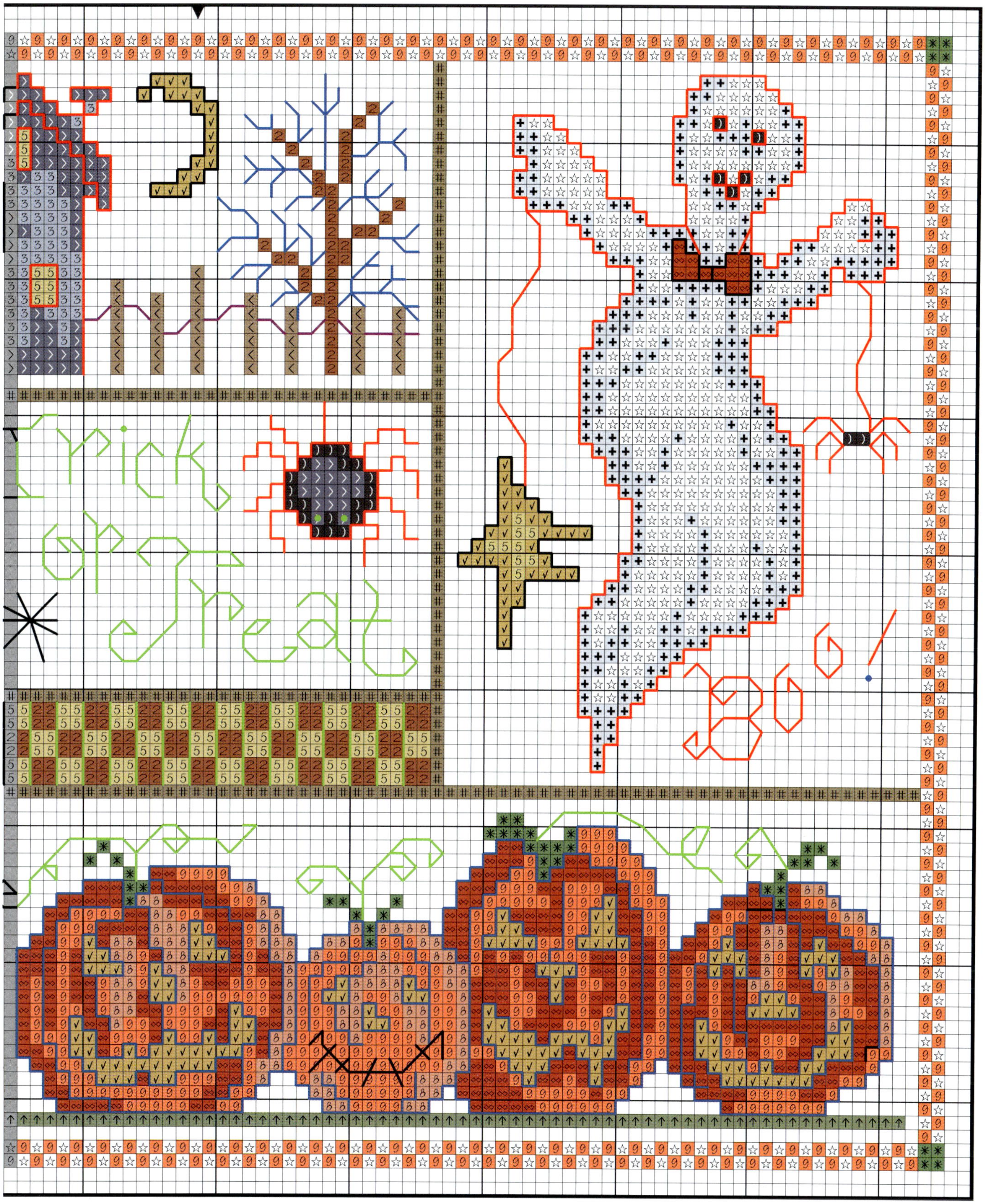

Let Us Give Thanks

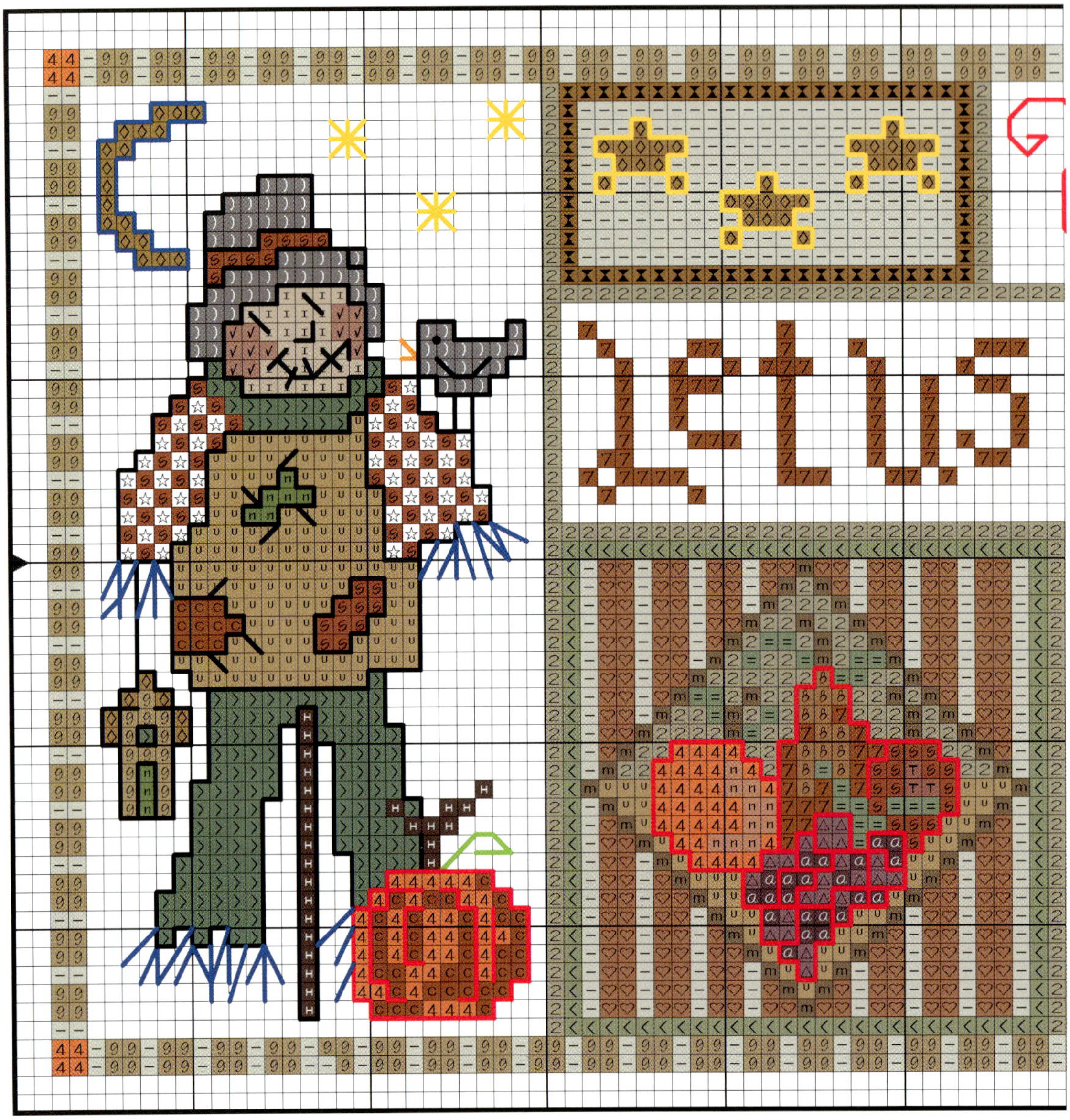

X	DMC	ANC.	COLOR
☆	blanc	2	white
–	ecru	387	ecru
>	320	215	green
+	368	214	lt green
♡	402	1047	lt burnt orange
)	413	236	grey
m	420	374	dk golden brown
9	422	943	lt golden brown
⧗	435	1046	brown
∧	437	362	lt brown
U	676	891	lt antique gold
2	677	886	vy lt antique gold

X	DMC	B'ST	ANC.	COLOR
	680	*/	901	dk antique gold
◊	729	/	890	antique gold
√	758		868	peach
H	801	/	359	dk brown
C	921		1003	dk orange
4	922		1003	orange
△	3041		871	purple
✳	3047		852	tan
n	3347		266	dk green
=	3363	/	262	olive
<	3364		260	lt olive
a	3740		873	dk purple

X	DMC	1/4X	B'ST	ANC.	COLOR
I	3774			778	lt peach
7	3776	7	/	1048	burnt orange
T	3778			1013	dk peach
X	3799		/	236	dk grey
L	3821			305	gold
┴	3822			295	lt gold
n	3825			323	orange
8	3827	8		311	straw
3	3828	3		373	golden brown
S	3830			5975	copper
•	3799			236	dk grey Fr. Knot
•	3830			5975	copper Fr. Knot

Grey area indicates last row of previous section of design.

* Use **2** strands of floss.

Design was stitched on a 15¼" x 10" piece of 28 count Natural Linen over two fabric threads (design size 9¼" x 4"). Three strands of floss were used for Cross Stitch and one strand for Backstitch and French Knots except where noted in key. The design was custom framed.

Stitch Count (128w x 56h)

14 count	9¼"	x	4"
16 count	8"	x	3½"
18 count	7¼"	x	3¼"

Noel

X	DMC	B'ST	ANC.	COLOR
☆	blanc	/	2	white
9	415		398	grey
$	436		1045	golden brown
∞	501		878	dk green
)	502		877	green
+	503		876	lt green
=	644		830	beige
I	676		891	gold
√	677		886	lt gold
U	729	/	890	dk gold
#	762		234	lt grey
>	822		390	lt beige
□	948		1011	tan
	3031	/	905	dk brown
♡	3790		393	brown
↑	3813		875	vy lt sea green
✱	3815		877	dk sea green
8	3816		876	sea green
♦♦	3831		29	pink
2	3832		28	lt pink
◇	3833		26	dk pink
●	501	/	878	dk green Fr. Knot
●	3031		905	dk brown Fr. Knot
●	3831		29	pink Fr. Knot

Grey area indicates last row of previous section of design.

The design was stitched on a 14" x 11½" piece of 28 count Confederate Grey Cashel Linen® over two fabric threads (design size 7¾" x 5¼"). Three strands of floss were used for Cross Stitch and one strand for Backstitch and French Knots. The design was custom framed.

Stitch Count (107w x 71h)

14 count	7¾"	x	5¼"
16 count	6¾"	x	4½"
18 count	6"	x	4"

Joys of the Season

X	DMC	$^1/_4$X	B'ST	ANC.	COLOR
☆	blanc	☆		2	white
8	347		/	1025	red
◆◆	501	◆	/	878	dk green
7	502			877	green
$	642			392	beige
~	676			891	gold
=	677			886	lt gold
+	729		/	890	dk gold
L	762			234	grey
■	844		/	1041	dk grey
o	922	o		1003	orange
√	926			850	blue grey

X	DMC	B'ST	ANC.	COLOR
/	948		1011	peach
I	3072		847	lt grey
9	3328		1024	dk pink
◇	3712		1023	pink
◇	3768		779	dk blue grey
	3781	/	904	dk brown
H	3782		899	lt brown
2	3790		393	brown
●	501		878	dk green Fr. Knot
●	844		1041	dk grey Fr. Knot
●	3328		1024	dk pink Fr. Knot

Grey area indicates last row of previous section of design.

The design was stitched on a 15" x 10 1/2" piece of 28 count Cream Linen over two fabric threads (design size 8 3/4" x 4 1/2"). Three strands of floss were used for Cross Stitch and one strand for Backstitch and French Knots. The design was custom framed.

Stitch Count (122w x 62h)

14 count	8 3/4"	x	4 1/2"
16 count	7 3/4"	x	4"
18 count	7"	x	3 1/2"

HOW TO READ CHARTS

Each chart is made up of a key and a gridded design on which each square represents a stitch. The symbols in the key tell which floss color to use for each stitch in the chart. The following headings and symbols are given:

X — Cross Stitch
DMC — DMC color number
1/4 X — Quarter Stitch
B'ST — Backstitch
ANC. — Anchor color number
COLOR — The name given to the floss color in this chart

A square filled with a color and a symbol should be worked as a **Cross Stitch**.

A triangle should be worked as a **Quarter Stitch**.

A straight line should be worked as a **Backstitch**.

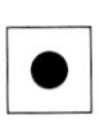

A large dot listed near the end of the key should be worked as a **French Knot**.

Sometimes the symbol for a Cross Stitch may be partially covered when a Backstitch crosses the square. Refer to the background color to determine the floss color.

HOW TO STITCH

Always work **Cross Stitches** and **Quarter Stitches** first and then add the **Backstitch** and **French Knots**. When stitching, bring the threaded needle up at 1 and all odd numbers and down at 2 and all even numbers.

Cross Stitch (X): For horizontal rows, work stitches in two journeys ***(Fig. 1)***. For vertical rows, complete each stitch as shown ***(Fig. 2)***. When working over two fabric threads, work Cross Stitch as shown in **Fig. 3**.

Fig. 1

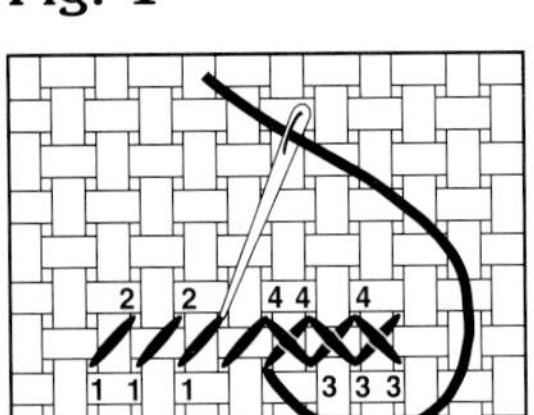

Fig. 2

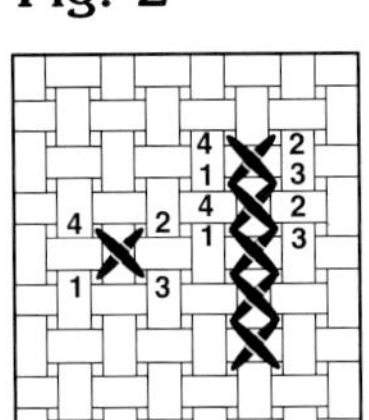

Fig. 3

Quarter Stitch (1/4X): Come up at 1 ***(Fig. 4)***, and then split the fabric thread to go down at 2. **Fig. 5** shows the technique for the Quarter Stitch when working over two fabric threads.

Fig. 4

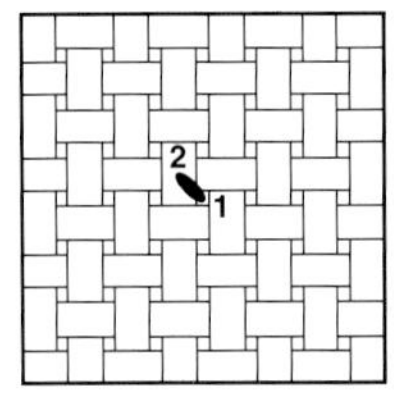

Fig. 5

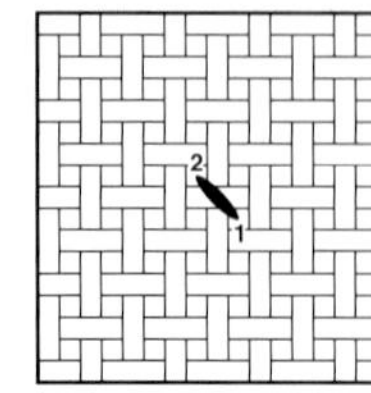

Backstitch (B'ST): For outlines and details, Backstitch should be worked after the design has been completed ***(Fig. 6)***. When working over two fabric threads, work the Backstitch as shown in **Fig. 7**.

Fig. 6

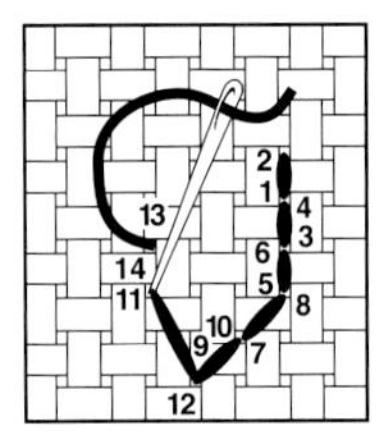

Fig. 7

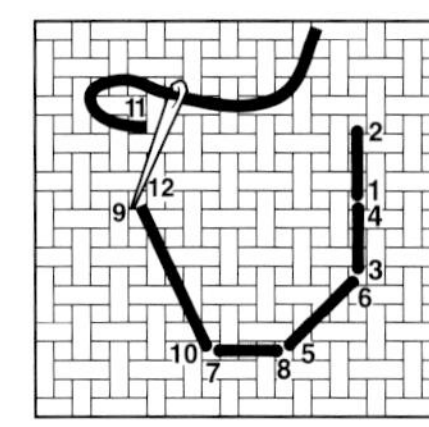

French Knot: Bring the needle up at 1. Wrap floss once around the needle. Insert the needle at 2, tighten the knot, and pull the needle through the fabric, holding the floss until it must be released ***(Fig. 8)***. For a larger knot, use more floss strands; wrap only once.

Fig. 8

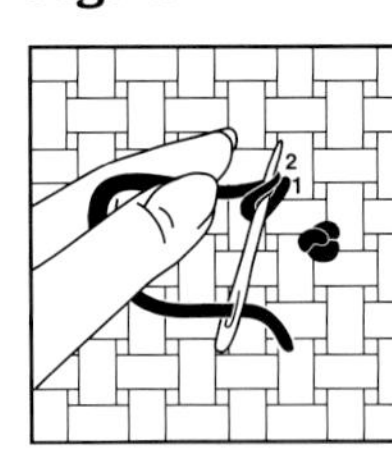